~~Becom~~ STAYING

a

Vegetarian

A Step-by-Step Guide to the Basics of Vegetarian
Cooking and the Required Ingredients to Start Making
Easy, Quick and Healthy Vegetarian Dishes

By Trent Joslin

Contents

Thank you for buying this book and I hope that you will find it useful. If you will want to share your thoughts on this book, you can do so by leaving a review on the Amazon page, it helps me out a lot.

Introduction

If you have actually consumed meat your entire life, going vegetarian may be a thing which may be challenging to switch to. You may additionally question why you ought to even think about switching. Lots of folks figure that they have been eating in this manner their entire life, so why change now?

There are lots of reasons why you may choose to change to a vegetarian diet. To start with, look at yourself in the mirror. Most Americans are not at a good weight and this could be the top reason for them to change. Additionally, ask yourself a couple of questions:

- Are you at a healthy weight?

- Do you feel great the majority of the time?

- Do you get up invigorated? Or exhausted and slow?

- How is your general health?

- Is your blood pressure in a healthy range?

- Are your blood sugar and cholesterol levels ordinary?

If you discover that "no" is the response to the majority of these questions, then you ought to think about what you are eating daily. If you discover that you feel worse after eating, you might be questioning if food should make you feel like this.

The response is no. Your food ought to feed and nourish your body. It ought to leave you feeling revitalized and invigorated. The body is a machine and it requires excellent fuel. The truth is that many folks are obese and overweight. This is since we eat excessive meat and excessive fat. Issues like Type II diabetes, high blood sugar, high cholesterol and other health-related issues are triggered by our diet. All of these issues could be avoided by altering your diet. This guide is going to show you how to do so, and the difference that eating like a vegetarian could do for you in a brief amount of time.

Chapter 1: What You Eat Matters

Whatever reasons you have for ending up being a vegetarian, there are 4 various kinds of vegetarians and you could pick the type which you wish to be. There are several kinds of vegetarians, as certain individuals are unable to quit all animal products totally. The 4 types are:

- Lacto Vegetarians: This diet includes no animal items or eggs. They do consume dairy products like milk, yogurt and cheese.

- Ovo-Vegetarians: This diet contains no dairy or animal, yet they do consume eggs.

- Lacto-Ovo Vegetarians: This diet is composed of no animal products, yet they do consume eggs and dairy.

- Vegan: This diet consists of plant-based foods, and that indicates that it leaves out all animal items involving dairy, meat, eggs, and even honey.

If you have not found out what kind of vegetarian you will be, it's alright. It requires time and experimentation with various recipes to determine what you can't do without. For instance, certain individuals can't live without eggs and milk.

You Truly are What You Eat

The expression "you are what you eat" has actually been heard various times, and it is frequently utilized in ads. However, if you truly consider what this suggests, you truly begin to reconsider your diet.

A fine instance of an individual being what they eat could be seen in your blood plasma. Your blood plasma is a clear fluid, yet after consuming a fast-food hamburger, your blood plasma ends up being cloudy with cholesterol and fat. This is what your body takes in after consuming a high-fat hamburger.

Inversely, you additionally end up being what you do not eat. When you shift from consuming a great deal of meat to consuming a vegetarian-based diet plan, you lose fat. You are additionally less susceptible to numerous diseases and cancers. Your cholesterol could additionally get better. When you are lean and consuming fewer meat items, you discover that a number of your health and fitness issues disappear. The Type II diabetes risk is additionally lowered. Blood pressure falls under regular ranges too. When you're much healthier, you additionally do not need to take as many medications.

If you have a family history of high blood pressure or high cholesterol, then you are especially dependent on what you eat, and it is simpler for you to become what you eat. Shifting to a vegetarian diet plan could lower the occurrence of various illnesses. Vegetarians are additionally statistically much healthier.

What Did Our Ancestors Eat?

Initially our ancestors were hunter-gatherers and not omnivores. They did not consume animals. When you check out carnivorous animals and predators, you could see that they have teeth made to rip and tear. Their teeth are not made for chewing. Animals which are made for chewing such as herbivores have flat teeth which are made to break food down.

People evolved from animals which were vegetarian. The digestive systems were not created for consuming and digesting meat. Eating meat is a relatively recent advancement in human history. It is thought that people started to consume meat since they could not discover the natural foods they were accustomed to consuming. They may have presumed that consuming meat would aid in sustaining their meat.

At first, we resembled animals that developed from animals such as herbivore apes. These apes appeared comparable to man and walked upright with their hands and arms. They scavenged for food naturally and ate berries, roots, nuts and fruits. They additionally lived second to second, continuously foraging for food. Hunting needs thought and eating meat needed fire. Up until fire was found, man mainly ate fruits and veggies. Vegetarian eating is a natural kind of eating and a lot healthier.

Why Did Human Beings Begin Eating Meat?

Prehistoric humans who resided in frozen locations consumed anything which they might to make it through. The prehistoric man needed to consume meat so as to stay alive. This would be the initial time that they had actually ever consumed meat. This changed how individuals would eat permanently.

The initial meat which was consumed would have been cooked by fire which was begun by natural forest fires. Without fire, they might have potentially eaten raw meat too. The digestive system more than probably rebelled to consuming the raw meat, yet as they ended up being adjusted, meat ended up being a part of their routine diets.

You might have heard of individuals who have actually lived vegetarian lives for an extended time period and after that ended up being strongly ill later. This is comparable to what prehistoric humans would have undergone. Biologists are going to tell you that we are not truly made to digest meat, yet that we have actually adjusted to it with time.

The Tradition of Consuming Meat

As men established, they started eating increasingly more meat. This resulted in entire families consuming meat as the primary portion of their meal and hence the tradition of consuming meat started. The turkey ended up being the Thanksgiving dinner staple. New Year's has actually always been connected with sauerkraut and pork. Ham is the conventional Easter meal. In the summertime, you can't wait to smell barbeque. As you consider all of the meat which we take in, it's tough to believe that we were made to live off of veggies, fruits, berries and nuts.

When people needed to start eating meat to stay alive, it ended up being a group occasion. One Indian was unable to head out and hunt a buffalo by himself. It took at least 4 individuals to hunt a buffalo. The identical holds true for a range of other animals which we hunted and ate. The meat ended up being the focal point and it took a number of tribe or family members to tidy, cook and even dry the meat. After the work was carried out, the meat was shared as a prize for hard work.

Now, we do not need to hunt our meat, but we do purchase it. We still take pleasure in getting together and celebrating with a ham, due to the fact that this is instilled in our nature from countless years of customs. All celebrations have a tendency to hover across some kind of food item, yet picture what your choices would be if we quit meat and envision just how much healthier our meals might be.

If you acknowledge that you might feel far better about yourself if you had the ability to eat healthier, then that ought to be a sufficient reason to change or at least reduce the quantity of meat which you consume. You do not need to make a total switch. Sure, certain individuals take pleasure in a good cold glass of milk and might require it to make certain they are getting ample vitamin D and calcium. If you do not think you could give meat up entirely, you could just make your meat more of a side dish and eat veggies. You are going to be surprised at the distinction it is going to make.

Chapter 2: Vegetarianism & Animal Well-being

Lots of vegetarians are such not only since they understand it is healthy, but for the reason of animal well-being too. For lots of folks, being a vegetarian is a part of an ethical and moral choice to not eat animal items. Across the numerous centuries, we have domesticated animals, we have come to think that we are superior to them. We utilize animals for a variety of utilizations besides food including shoes, clothing, coats and belts. They have actually additionally been utilized for scientific experiments, even though lots of firms are attempting to move far from this kind of testing.

PETA

PETA is an organization which is committed to altering the attitude of individuals when it pertains to animals. They are versus utilizing animals for everything from clothing to food, and they are especially in opposition to trapping for fur.

PETA is very enthusiastic about their cause, practically to the extent of being outrageous. Nevertheless, their cause is worthy because they think animals have rights and deserve that their best interests are taken into account. They seek to have individuals understand that animals are able to suffer and that they are interested in leading their own lives as animals. They think that as a society, we have to re-evaluate our position on earth and where we fit in with the other animal residers of the planet.

Animals & Growth Hormones

In an attempt to make more animals at an accelerated rate for human intake, numerous animals have actually been injected with growth hormones so that they could be raised and butchered at an expedited rate. Simultaneously, this leads us to think about how these animals are treated and raised for this goal.

The truth is that if plenty of individuals saw how many of these animals were raised, they would end up being vegetarians right there. For instance, egg-laying chicken are typically raised with 6 other chicken in a cage. Every chicken just gets around 67 square inches of room. These chickens are additionally typically injected with growth hormones in addition to antibiotics to boost growth rate and reduce disease. Free-range and licensed organic chickens might get more roomy conditions and are not fed antibiotics or hormones.

This brings us to one more point. After you deal with chickens, it is recommended that you utilize bleach to clean up the surfaces to ensure that you get rid of bacteria. Additionally, the chicken need to be cooked at particular temperatures and for a particular time period to guarantee that you are not going to catch any food-borne diseases. It does not appear smart to eat anything which needs to be handled with care like that.

From chickens, you could quickly move into how cattle are treated. Initially, you need to consider dairy cattle. Dairy cattle are frequently provided with hormones which promote their reproductive processes so that it keeps on producing milk. A cow is going to just generate milk after she has delivered. They typically reside in cramped conditions, and as quickly as they calve, male calves are sent out to end up being veal while females are raised to generate milk. The hormones which the cows get induce the cow to produce 10 times more milk than they would generally. Simultaneously, they are linked to electric pumps, which result in irritation to the cow's udders.

After a particular age, we truly do not have to consume milk. Simultaneously, we are not made to consume cow milk, but human milk. We do not milk pregnant women, do we? Similar to our bodies were not made to consume milk, we were not made to consume cow milk and digest those proteins. You could get just as much and more calcium from leafy, green veggies.

Plenty of individuals, even those individuals who eat meat frequently, have actually seen the veal industry adversely. The veal market is terrible regardless of how you look at it and who you are. The calves are taken from their mothers after they are around a day old. They are then kept in pens which stop movement so that their muscle tissue remains tender and soft. The calves are then fed a liquid, frequently consisting of beer, which lacks fiber and iron. This results in anemia in the animal and results in pale meat. At around 20 weeks, the calf is then butchered.

Turkeys are additionally produced in a cruel way. The turkey consumption has actually ended up being incredibly prominent over the past couple of decades, and it is eaten for more than only holidays. Turkeys are more aggressive birds, so they are placed in a caged and dark place to dissuade their aggressive habits. They are then overfed up until their legs can not support their bodyweight. This is since Americans desire the biggest turkey breast they are able to get for their holiday parties. Wildly and naturally , a turkey might live up to ten years. These turkeys are butchered at 2 years of age. They additionally deal with leg and foot deformities, heat stress and hunger. Roughly 2.7 million turkeys perish every year because of the abnormal stress and illness of this procedure.

Lots of religions do not eat pork for their different reasons and certain meat-consuming individuals don't care for it either. Pigs are raised in comparable unhygienic conditions. Actually, lots of workers and farmers on pig farms have actually died from inhaling the methane gas which is produced from the enormous quantity of waste which pigs create at pig farms. Pigs are additionally kept in cages and overfed. They have a minimal range of motion which does not match their natural behaviors. They might additionally be fed antibiotics and growth hormones. Pigs have natural rooting behaviors, and the captivity they reside in does not let them live naturally.

Shellfish and seafood could be an aspect of a healthy diet. Fish consist of a great deal of nutrients which we do not receive from other meats. It consists of a top-quality protein, important nutrients, omega-3 fatty acids and it is low in saturated fat. Nevertheless, consuming fish has its harms too. Fish typically include mercury. These levels are not typically sufficiently bad to harm us, yet the Environmental Protection Agency (EPA) and the Food and Drug Administration (FDA) are encouraging ladies, specifically pregnant ladies, and young kids to stay away from specific kinds of shellfish and fish. This is due to the fact that some fish have high mercury levels which are not safe for these individuals to consume. Removing fish from your diet is generally the final step in going towards an entirely vegetarian diet.

Chapter 3: Vegetarianism & The Health Impacts

You are going to be certainly astonished at the distinction you feel when you have eaten meat for a brief time period. It's as if your body immediately starts to alleviate itself of all of the contaminants which you have actually been taking in, and you instantly start to feel more invigorated and have a general better sense of health.

Regardless of your reasons for consuming a more vegetarian diet, the health benefits which are obtained are going to end up being apparent in a really brief quantity of time. Vegetarians have a tendency to have cholesterol, lower blood fats, and triglycerides than meat eaters of comparable status and age. Even those vegetarians who eat milk and eggs rapidly see that their cholesterol is lower than those individuals who consume meat.

Heart Disease

High blood fats levels are connected with an increased risk of cardiovascular disease. Researchers have actually discovered that men who consume meat six or more times weekly double their odds of cultivating heart disease. Middle-aged men are more probable to deal with deadly heart attacks. Ladies are shielded by their hormones for most of their life, yet older ladies are susceptible to establish heart disease later on in life. Older ladies who are vegetarians have actually been demonstrated to have a lower risk of cardiovascular disease.

In 1982, British researchers carried out a study on more than 10,000 meat-eaters and vegetarians. They discovered that the more meat that was taken in, the higher the risk of a cardiac arrest. They additionally discovered that by getting rid of meat from your diet, you are decreasing your consumption of cholesterol and fats which are harming the heart. Simultaneously, nevertheless, you need to make sure not to make up for not eating meat by consuming excessive eggs and milk, as this could negate the advantages. To get all of the vegetarianism benefits, your intake of ice cream, cream cheese, hard cheese, and eggs must be moderate. The introduction of more fruits, veggies, and raw foods is going to improve your benefits.

Cancer

Vegetarianism has actually additionally been demonstrated to minimize the occurrence of particular kinds of cancer too. These diets are high in fiber, low in saturated fat, and consist of phytochemicals, that shield from cancer. Numerous big studies in both Germany and England have actually revealed that vegetarians, when compared to meat-eaters, have around a 40% less chance of cultivating cancer in comparison to meat-eaters. Seventh-Day Adventists are mainly lacto-ovo vegetarians and have been recognized to have a decreased cancer risk due to the fact that they have a tendency to stay away from meat. In China, it has actually been discovered that they have similarly lowered breast cancer rates as a result of the quantity of veggies which they consume. On the other hand, Japanese women have a tendency to consume more meat and are 8 times more probable to cultivate breast cancer.

Dairy and meat consumption has been connected to different other cancers involving:

- Colon cancer

- Prostate cancer

- Ovarian cancer

In studies performed by Harvard on numerous thousand women, it has been discovered that those who routinely consume meat boost their odds of colon cancer by 300%. These high-fat diets which plenty of individuals consume additionally induce the body to create excess estrogen. This boost has been connected to increased odds of breast cancer. They have additionally discovered that breast cancer rates are one third greater in premenopausal women who consume meat diets primarily.

Cambridge University has additionally connected meat diets with high levels of saturated fat to breast cancer. They have connected dairy items to an increased ovarian cancer risk as the procedure of breaking down lactose might harm the ovaries. In men, prostate enhancement has been connected to meat intake, and the danger triples.

Other studies have actually connected a boost in white blood cell production to vegetarianism too. These cells are needed in warding off infection, bacteria, and illness. Hence, the immunity is more powerful when a vegetarian diet is consumed.

Improved Digestion

Vegetarians see a great deal of improvement in their digestion since they have the ability to generate a natural and healthy environment for these organs. Our digestive system was initially created to consume more veggie matter instead of meat. Fruits, legumes, veggies, and nuts were the staple of the prehistoric diet and your digestive system considerably benefits when you return to this natural kind of diet plan. The Western diet has been dramatically altered to consist of extremely processed food and refined sugar and flour items.

This has actually resulted in a range of health issues from cardiovascular disease to weight problems.

When the body isn't being fed effectively and the digestion isn't working appropriately, the body starts to adapt. It starts to make changes in the cells of the colon and stomach. When we do not consume ample fiber, we incur a range of issues, including hemorrhoids and constipation. These issues are not typically seen in a vegetarian diet.

Weight

Weight is a big issue in this nation, and if you think of it, have you ever truly seen a fat vegetarian? Probably you have not. Actually, a lot of vegetarians are healthy and lean. Any time you see a nutritionist or dietician, they probably tell you to boost your veggie consumption and reduce the quantity of meat you consume, particularly pork and red meats. Lots of vegetarians who resume their old diets have actually discovered that the weight they lost has a tendency to return. Your will power is insufficient to prevent the weight gain from consuming a high-fat meat-based diet.

You are naturally much healthier and feel greater when you consume a diet plan which is high in dietary fiber, which is taken in from fruits and veggies. As a vegetarian, you are basically feeding your body the nutrition which it requires to supply your body with beneficial energy, not energy which needs to be kept. You simply feel much better due to this.

Lots of diets stop working since we are pushing ourselves to stay away from the food which we like. This just causes the temptation to consume those foods. The secret to being an effective vegetarian is to understand that you do not need to consume meat and that you could go without it. You are concentrated on consuming much healthier and you forget that you are attempting to drop weight. You really start to drop weight without understanding it, merely since you have actually removed your primary source of fat and general unhealthiness. Simultaneously, all of the bad health impacts vanish due to your natural and healthy diet.

Kidneys

Diet plans that are high in animal proteins have a tendency to trigger the body to excrete more uric acid, calcium, and oxalates. These are 3 compounds which are the primary elements of kidney stones. For those individuals who tend to get kidney stones, British scientists have actually encouraged that these individuals follow a vegetarian diet plan. The American Academy of Household Physicians has actually likewise validated that high animal protein usage is the reason for kidney stones in the United States too. By consuming a vegetarian diet plan your body does not produce as much of these compounds; for that reason, it does not form kidney stones.

Osteoporosis

For a number of the identical reasons we have the ability to minimize the kidney stone risk by consuming a vegetarian diet plan, we are additionally able to decrease our odds of osteoporosis. Consuming meat might really promote bone loss due to the fact that it pushes calcium out of the body. In lots of countries where veggies are the foundation of their diet, osteoporosis is less prevalent than in industrialized nations such as the United States. Calcium is also consumed less in the United States.

So, with our meat-eating diet plans, we are pressed to additionally take in calcium supplements and prescription drugs to protect against the start of osteoporosis. These supplements could additionally have extreme side effects. Lots of nutrition specialists acknowledge that the calcium supplements acquired at drug shops are inferior to the calcium that you get from natural food sources. This is generally due to the fact that they are not absorbed effectively by the body.

There are a number of excellent calcium sources consisting of:

- Dry beans

- Orange juice

- Tofu.

- Dark leafy veggies

Detoxing

Plenty of individuals have actually gotten on a kick of doing weekend Detox diets and comparable programs. Did you know that you do not need to do this if you are a vegetarian? Cleansing the body of damaging toxic substances is simple if you consume a vegetarian diet. You are not taking in all of the antibiotics and growth hormones that you receive from the meat that you buy at the supermarket. Individuals actually do not recognize that they get these toxins from their carnivorous diet plan. A diet which is high in processed foods and fat has a tendency to decelerate the digestion of your food and this enables your body to absorb and build up the toxic substances from this kind of diet.

Bacteria and toxic substances which build up in your system could additionally develop a sensation of sluggishness. There are additionally a range of digestive conditions, like colitis and irritable bowel disorders which might develop too. When you consume a healthy vegetarian diet, you introduce dietary fiber to your diet plan and your gastrointestinal system starts to quickly work much better.

When you remove meat from your diet, your body is devoid of the extreme work it requires to digest those kinds of food. All appears to end up being clearer and work much better. You additionally end up being more aware of the food toxicity you had been consuming previously.

Chemicals and toxic substances in our food have actually ended up being a big concern in the United States. There are a growing number of preservatives and chemicals being included to our food. We are consuming these products each time we consume refined foods, processed foods, and numerous other antibiotics and hormones which we get through our meat. Due to this, a range of other problems are created in its wake consisting of:

- Cancer

- Heart disease

- Arthritis

- Diabetes

- Weight problems

- Skin issues

- Headaches

- Tiredness

- Discomforts

- Coughs

- Intestinal issues

- Weak body immune systems

Chapter 4: Making the Change

If you are thinking about making a change to a vegetarian diet plan, you most likely are going to wish to pass your newly found dietary knowledge onto your family. Actually, as a parent, you most likely wish to make sure that your household is getting the ideal nutrition feasible. It additionally aids them to discover why it is necessary to eat healthily.

Making the change with a family could be hard since kids are a lot more tempted from the numerous fast-food restaurants and commercials for treats on tv. It's really tough to make veggies seem great over chicken nuggets and a complimentary toy!

You need to alter your family's diet gradually. All begins at the supermarket. Rather than cookies, purchase bananas, apples, carrots and other delicious treats. Exchange white rice for brown, healthy rice. You additionally wish to stay clear of processed side dishes. Gradually make your meat servings tinier and add more grains and veggies. In case you have kids, it is a lot easier to make this change. You could teach them from an early age that olives are excellent treats and that peaches are great desserts. They are going to learn to enjoy these foods and they will not even find out about all the other unhealthy foods out there. The actual obstacle is going to come when your kids are in school, and they need to learn to make healthy choices.

The idea is to slowly change so that it is less troublesome on you and your household. Numerous kids are going to change just since you tell them that they are saving animals' lives. Kids are extremely understanding and it's not uncommon for kids to end up being vegetarians by themselves merely since they do not wish to consume animals.

Your kids might not understand it now, yet you are doing them a big favor which is going to last them their whole lives. Youth obesity is at epidemic levels in the United States and you are going to be setting your kids up for a healthy way of life by teaching them how to eat healthily.

Things You Require to Begin Cooking Vegetarian Style

You are going to utilize the identical kind of cooking items that you currently utilize. Nevertheless, you might want to break out the food processor and the blender if you aren't utilizing it regularly.

There are likewise numerous brand-new ingredients and foods which you are going to be including into your diet plan consisting of:

Fruits & Veggies

- Melon
- Grapes
- Mushrooms
- Apple
- Tomatoes
- Avocado
- Broccoli

- Oranges
- Potato
- Kiwi
- Peppers
- Sweet Potato
- Onion
- Cucumber
- Cherry
- Celery
- Carrot
- Plum
- Banana
- Cabbage

Egg Whites, Soy Milk & Dairy (Unless You Are Giving These Up)

- Milk
- Egg whites
- Soy Milk
- Dairy Milk
- Soy Cheese
- Dairy Cheese
- Yogurt

Sauces & Oils

- Rice vinegar
- Olive oil
- Groundnut oil
- Toasted Sesame Oil
- Hot Chili Oil
- Tamari (Japanese Soy Sauce)

Seasonings

- Curry Powder
- Black Pepper
- Fresh Garlic
- Dijon Mustard
- Sea Salt
- Fresh Ginger

Herbs & Spices

- Basil
- Anise
- Chili powder
- Cayenne pepper
- Coriander
- Cinnamon
- Dill
- Cumin
- Nutmeg
- Garlic powder
- Paprika
- Oregano
- Rosemary
- Red chili flakes
- Thyme
- Sage

Noodles & Rice

- Soba noodles
- Rice noodles

- Brown basmati rice

Nuts & Seeds

- Cashews
- Almonds
- Sesame Seeds
- Peanuts
- Sunflower seeds

Legumes

- Chickpeas
- Black beans
- Split Peas (Green and yellow)
- Lentils (Red, brown and green)
- Kidney beans

Other

- Nutritional yeast
- Coconut milk
- Raw, unrefined sugar
- Pure Maple Syrup

Breakfast & Brunch

Breakfast is an essential meal which plenty of individuals skip. The truth is that if you eat at least your 3 standard meals daily, you are going to really drop weight, if that is your objective. Additionally, it does not need to be uninteresting and dull, and vegetarians have a couple of delicious choices.

Apple Cinnamon Granola

Ingredients

- 1 cup wheat germ
- 4 cups oatmeal
- dash of nutmeg
- 1 tsp. ground cinnamon
- 1/2 cup honey
- 1/2 cup finely sliced walnuts
- 1 cup dried apples, finely sliced
- 2 tbsp. Sunflower oil
- 1/2 cup raisins

Preheat oven to 275 degrees Fahrenheit. In a big blending bowl, combine wheat germ, oatmeal, nutmeg, cinnamon, and walnuts. In a different bowl, mix sunflower oil and honey and drizzle across the top of the mix. Mix together, whisking continuously, up until the oat mix is uniformly covered with oil and honey. Gently oil a big baking sheet and spread out the mix over the pan. Bake for thirty minutes, whisking every 10 minutes. As soon as the granola turns golden, extract from the oven and put aside to cool. Prepare jars to put the prepared granola in. When cool, include dried apples and raisins and move the mix into jars. Stock in a dry location.

Produces 6 cups.

Simple Crepes

Ingredients

- 3/4 cup + 2 tbsp. All-purpose flour
- 3 eggs
- 1 tbsp. Granulated sugar
- 1 1/2 cups milk
- Pinch salt
- 1 tbsp. Vegetable oil
- Whip cream, for the filling
- 1 tsp. Butter
- A couple of handfuls of raspberries, rinsed and drained
- A couple of handfuls of strawberries washed with stems removed and cut in half
- A couple of handfuls of blueberries, rinsed and drained

Mix eggs, milk, flour, oil, sugar, and salt in food processor or a blender. Mix up until smooth. Transfer batter into a blending bowl, cover and put aside in the fridge for at least thirty minutes. Include the butter into a non-stick skillet across medium-high heat. As soon as the butter has actually melted, include 1/4 cup of the batter into the pan and swirl around to coat the entire bottom of the pan. Cook up until the crepe gently browns, around 1 or 2 minutes. Turn over and cook the 2nd side up until browned lightly. Move to plates and spray a line of whip cream down the center. Sprinkle in your fruit. Fold the sides delicately to create a cylinder.

Produces 8 to 12 crepes

Vegetable Omelet

Ingredients

- 3 tbsp. Milk
- 2 eggs
- Large pinch of black pepper
- Large pinch of salt
- 1/4 c. green bell pepper

- 1 tbsp. Butter
- 1/4 c. Onion
- 1/4 c. red bell pepper
- Grated cheese to taste (optional).

In a medium-size blending bowl, beat salt, eggs, pepper, red and green pepper and onion with a fork. Do not over mix. Melt the butter in a 7 to 8-inch pan across medium-high heat. Make certain the butter covers the foundation of the pan. When the foam isn't there any more, pour in the egg mix. Tilt the pan to make certain the egg covers the whole foundation of the pan. Allow the eggs to sit for 45 seconds prior to turning. Do the identical on the other side. When done, move to a plate and sprinkle with cheese.

Smoothies

Smoothies are fantastic and extremely healthy. You could have them as treats or drink them with your breakfast.

Breakfast Smoothies

Ingredients

- 3 to 4 bananas
- 1 1/2 cups plain fat-free yogurt
- 1/4 cup soy milk
- 3 cups of strawberries, stems taken out and roughly sliced
- 1 cup of ice
- 2 tbsp. Honey

Mix ingredients into blender one by one and offer.

Yogurt and Banana Smoothie

Ingredients

- 1 cup low-fat plain or vanilla yogurt
- 1 ripe banana, very finely sliced

- 3/4 cup skim milk

Put aside 2 or 3 pieces of banana and put the remainder of the banana in the blender. Include milk and yogurt. Mix up until smooth and garnish with additional banana pieces and a dash of cinnamon.

Mango Smoothie

Ingredients

- 1 peeled banana
- 1 mango, peeled and sliced
- 1 tsp. Honey
- 3 tbsp. Yogurt
- 4 ice cubes
- 1/2 tsp. cinnamon

Put ingredients in a blender one by one and puree up until smooth.

Pear Smoothie

Ingredients

- 1/2 inch fresh ginger
- 3 pears
- 1/2 tsp. Cinnamon
- 3 tbsp. Fresh yogurt
- 4 ice cubes

Slowly juice the ginger, pear, and cinnamon together. Move to a blender and include ice and yogurt. Mix up until smooth.

Appetizers & Side Dishes

These make fantastic sides to a well-balanced meal or an appetizer. You may even wish one for a treat!

Special Tomato Bruschetta

Ingredients

- 4 garlic cloves
- 4 bread rolls
- 1 tbsp. Sliced basil
- 4 big tomatoes
- 2 tbsp. Butter
- 8 black olives, pitted and cut in half
- 1 tbsp. Tomato paste
- Pepper and salt to taste
- 1 3/4 ounce mozzarella cheese, cut
- 2 tsp. lemon juice or Balsamic Vinegar
- 1 tbsp. Olive oil
- Basil leaves for garnish
- 1 tsp. clear honey

Put rolls on cutting board and cut every one in half. Move to a oven or toaster oven to crisp and brown. Preheat oven to 300 degrees Fahrenheit. Put garlic, butter and sliced basil into a little blending bowl and whisk up until mixed. When rolls are toasted, spoon garlic mix onto every half.

Pour boiling water into a big bowl, cut a little cross shape at the base of every tomato and put in boiling water. After tomatoes soften, take out and peel the flesh away from the tomatoes. When the flesh is removed, slice into little squares. Put diced tomatoes and olives in blending bowl and mix together. Spoon onto rolls.

In a different bowl, combine lemon juice, olive oil, and honey together. Drizzle mix across tomato covered rolls and lightly put mozzarella pieces on top. Sprinkle with pepper and salt. Put rolls on a baking sheet and put in the oven. Melt cheese for approximately 2 minutes.

Move rolls to a tray or plate and garnish with basil leaves.

Spring Rolls

Spring Rolls Ingredients

- 6 fresh shitake mushrooms
- 3/4 cup broken rice vermicelli noodles
- 1 cup bok choy, finely sliced
- 1/2 cup carrots, slivered
- 2 tbsp. Sliced coriander
- 1 cup green onion, slivered
- 2 tbsp. Soy sauce
- salt and ground pepper to taste
- 1 tsp. sesame oil
- 1/2 tsp. granulated sugar
- Eight 8 inch square spring roll skins
- 2 tsp. sliced fresh ginger
- 1/4 cup water
- 3 tbsp. All-purpose flour
- 4 cups vegetable oil

Salad Ingredients

- 1 cup carrots, slivered
- 1 cup daikon radish, slivered
- 1/2 cup red onion, slivered
- 4 green onions, slivered
- 1 cup slivered cucumber, juice squeezed out

Dressing Ingredients

- 1 tbsp. Soy sauce
- 2 tbsp. Seasoned rice vinegar
- 1/2 tsp. sesame oil

Put mushrooms and noodles into particular bowls and cover with boiling water. Cover bowls and put aside for 20 minutes. As soon as mushrooms and noodles have actually soaked, move to colander and drain. Move into a big bowl. Drain mushrooms too and move onto a cutting board. Remove and dispose of stems and cut mushroom heads finely. Include into a big bowl with noodles.

Include carrots, green onion, bok choy, and coriander into the bowl of mushrooms and noodles and blend together. Sprinkle in pepper, salt, and toss the mix to combine. Cover and put aside.

Put sugar, soy sauce, fresh ginger and sesame oil into a little bowl. Whisk the mix to combine properly. Cover and put aside.

Delicately pull spring roll skins apart and put on a flat, tidy surface area. Utilizing a little spoon, put 1/4 cup of the noodle and veggie mix onto the upper third of every skin. Roll one time, and after that, take the two ends and fold them in and keep on rolling the skins forward up until it forms a cylinder. Whisk flour together and water in a bowl up until properly mixed. Utilizing a little pastry brush, coat spring roll with simply ample water and flour mix to seal the edges. Repeat with every roll.

In a wok, heat a bit of the vegetable oil across medium-high heat. As soon as the oil and wok are hot, put spring rolls in 3 at once. Fry up until golden brown. Move onto a rack with a paper towel to drain.

To make the salad, put the carrot, radish, red and green onions and cucumber in a bowl and toss together. In a different bowl, pour in soy sauce, vinegar, and sesame oil. Blend together up until blended. When spring rolls are drained, put onto a cutting board and cut each in half at an angle. Serve 3 halves onto the plates standing with the cut ends up. Garnish with salad around rolls.

Main Courses

Pita Pizza

Ingredients

- 1/2 little onion, peeled and sliced and diced
- 1/4 tsp. olive oil
- 1/4 tsp. dried oregano
- 1 clove garlic, minced and peeled

- 1/4 tsp. crushed red pepper flakes
- 1/4 tsp. dried basil
- 1/2 cup tomato paste
- 1/2 cup canned entire peeled tomatoes, roughly sliced
- 1/2 yellow bell pepper, membranes and seeds removed, sliced into thin strips
- 2 whole-wheat pita bread
- 1/2 cup grated mozzarella cheese
- 1/8 cup baby spinach leaves, sliced into fine pieces
- Fresh basil, finely cut for garnish

Preheat oven to 350 degrees Fahrenheit. Across medium heat, heat oil in a skillet. Include garlic and onion, whisking periodically so that they do not burn. Cook for around 4 minutes up until both are brown. Sprinkle basil, oregano, bay leaf and red pepper flakes. Blend spices together. Whisk in tomato paste and peeled tomatoes, increase to high heat. When boiling, bring the heat to medium-low and enable the mix to simmer up until sauce is thick. Set up pizzas on baking sheets. Split sauce between pitas, leaving a crust border. Sprinkle mozzarella cheese on top. Bake in the oven for 20-25 minutes.

Chinese Noodles with Various Veggies

Sauce Ingredients

- 1 cup veggie stock
- 1 tsp. corn flour
- 2 tbsp. Rice wine
- 2 tbsp. Soy sauce
- 1 tsp. Sugar
- 1 tsp. salt

Noodles

- 12 oz. egg noodles

Vegetable Stir-Fry

- 1 clove garlic, finely sliced
- 3 tbsp. Sunflower oil

- 2 shallots, finely sliced
- 1-inch piece fresh ginger root, grated
- 250 g package Pak Choi, cut
- 1/4 cup button mushrooms, finely sliced
- 2 carrots, chopped into match sticks
- 1/2 cup bean sprouts

In a medium blending bowl, dissolve corn flour with a little quantity of vegetable stock in hot water. When dissolved, pour in rice wine, soy sauce, sugar and salt. Stir together up until well mixed or up until sugar liquifies.

Bring a big pot of water to a boil and include noodles. Cook up until tender. Move to a colander, drain appropriately and put in the pot. Put aside and maintain warm up until prepared to offer.

Put a big skillet or wok across medium-high heat and include the sunflower oil. When the oil is heated, include sliced garlic, shallots and ginger root. Allow it to sauté for a couple of seconds. Include mushrooms, bean sprouts, pak choi, and carrots and stir-fry for 1 to 2 minutes. Drizzle in sauce and proceed to stir-fry up until sauce thickens. Split noodles into various serving plates and top with veggie mix.

I hope that you enjoyed reading through this book and that you have found it useful. If you want to share your thoughts on this book, you can do so by leaving a review on the Amazon page. Have a great rest of the day.

Printed in Great Britain
by Amazon

13707898R00038